Enrique Blanco Joachim
A WARRIOR
of Life

authorHOUSE

AuthorHouse™
1663 Liberty Drive
Bloomington, IN 47403
www.authorhouse.com
Phone: 833-262-8899

Published by AuthorHouse 05/03/2022

ISBN: 978-1-6655-5895-2 (sc)
ISBN: 978-1-6655-5896-9 (e)

Library of Congress Control Number: 2022908473

Print information available on the last page.

Contents

Dedication

This book is dedicated, first of all, to God, for being the central pivot of my life; then to my dear mother, Rose Altagracia Joachim, for having instilled in me the values that I am characterized by as a person; to my siblings, Katiana Joachim (The Lawyer), Johanny Joachim (El Negru de la Bachata), and Yuberkis Altagracia Joachim; and to my friends, Luis Felipe Nez, Junior Tejada, Lisanna Mara Daz Payams, IdaniaPaulinoAdames (My Little Hand), Gerald Lee, JeantolbertJoassaint, Joan Rodrguez Nez, JenniferValdez, Francisco Luciano, MithoDoss, and a remaining list of countless people who, if I continued citing, there would be no more space left to put their names. In addition to all these people previously mentioned, I must also highlight that this book will be very useful to all those who seek to excel.

Special Thanks to:

American Accent English School-AAES
Cafeteria and dining in the Historic Center
César Cambio "CM"
Cafeteray copiadora Olga
Dr. Harlim-Kardosch
Dr. Vahid Nouri Kandany:
Dr. Rafael Ventura Iglesias.
The Consulate General of Haiti in Santiago,
Dominican Republic

We all have a story. Here is mine.

I was born surrounded by poverty, and I have only had the warmth of the moon, the stars, my family, and my friends. During my early adolescence, I started being taught at the best university in the world: life. At the same time, I have been doing what I think is correct, and at the same time, it makes me feel fulfilled. I have never tried to understand the meaning of life; I've just been living it. I've never looked back. I know I could not solve anything. I will firmly keep looking forward, because I know what I'm looking for.

Foreword

I met Doctor Enrique Blanco Joachim some years ago. On that occasion, there was no time to deepen our friendship, but I immediately noticed that there was something very special about him. What struck me the most during our short encounter was the aspiration and determination of that young man. When you finish reading this book, you will understand what I mean. He is a warrior and has a mission to fulfill. As a writer, dedicated to helping people overcome the obstacles they face in their lives and teaching them to achieve their goals using internal values, I feel content to have met Dr. Blanco, whose career and life teaching are motivating. I'm struck by that great man, his solid humility, his immense knowledge and interest in sharing his wisdom with others, his generosity and the passion to fulfill his mission no matter what may happen in the attempt. Reading this book and the application of this knowledge will produce remarkable changes in the lives of the readers. I affirm it because, in the first place, the book is based on a real life event. Everything that is narrated has been lived by a human being, a young fighter whose childhood has been very, very difficult. He has not given up, even facing the bitterest vicissitudes of life. In second place, Enrique's story will provoke an introspection that leads you to reflect on your own life, which generates responses to the deeper questions we might have. Anyway, I'm talking about a friend, brother, master, fighter, and warrior who is tracing a map to help others look for success. I must emphasize that readers will have the opportunity to have a suggestive guide book in their hands, whose content will become a source of inspiration to stand still and focus.

Ernst Cenege
Author of "Be More to a Better You"

Introduction

This book tells the story of a persevering young man, whose childhood has been very difficult and who, despite everything, has not let himself be overcome by the vicissitudes of life.

Speaking of personal improvement, I am talking about this new fighter, whose experiences are contained in this book, experiences that undoubtedly touch any human soul, and that is the reason why the reader will be able to understand life from a different perspective after reading through this powerful and life-changing story.

Reading this pleasant and sincere bunch of experiences is like being consubstantial with its author; it is like thinking: What would we do instead? Would we have had more and better alternatives or simply let time answer these questions?

Dear reader, after turning all the pages of this book, you will only have to act with humility and perseverance, and victory is assured. If you assimilate the essence of these reflections and assume them as a lesson in life, you will be prepared to achieve all your goals and aspirations.

In Ecclesiastes 7: 8, the Bible clearly states: "The end of a matter is better than its beginning, and patience is better than pride."

We live in a constant struggle to improve ourselves, but sometimes the question arises of whether all this effort is worth it.

What do you want to be in life? What do you want to achieve?

CHAPTER 1
YOU CAN!
NEVER GIVE UP!
ALWAYS BE HUMBLE!

These are three of my best phrases to start the day. I am the product of my mind (I am what I think). If I think that I am big and important, then without a doubt, it will be like that. In the same way, if I think that I am clumsy, a failure, or a loser, so it will be, because I am creating a mental image of myself and that will be the true reflection of what I think. A positive thought produces a positive action, but a negative thought produces a negative action.

Evidently, choosing to think positively would be the best option.

My life, like most people born in marginalized places and poverty, has not been easy. I was born in a community called *"batey"* (it is a poor area occupied by homes and other buildings in the sugar mills of the Caribbean). With the name *"batey"*, you can begin to conceive a mental image of the daily experience of those who live there. Due to the economic situation, I had to grab a box of shoeshine at 12 years of age in order to start working as a shoe cleaner, since I never had any help from my father and my mother was the one who was doing everything.

It does not matter where and how you start, but where and how you end up. We must not fear the circumstance of falling into misfortune.

Despite all that, I never stopped going to school. At the age of 15, I was already an expert shoeshine boy. Later on, I became a bus collector until I was 18 years old. Afterwards, I got my first formal job as a sales representative in a call center.

My story is not my destiny. Your story is not your destiny. If your past was not pleasant, then use it as a life experience and start your journey to a new future.

Do not let anyone tell you that you are too young to become someone in life.

A teacher once told me that life was not going to smile on me like it did on my brother. By then, he was very passionate about languages (no wonder he worked as a supervisor at a five-star hotel in the Dominican Republic). She always saw me reading and studying. It is possible that this caused her some discomfort; I never allowed the negative voices to penetrate beyond my ears.

In my last school year, I represented Puerto Plata (a city from my birth country) in Santo Domingo (the capital of D.R) in the "National Contest of Spelling Televised" and sponsored by the Vice President of the Dominican Republic, Dr. Margarita Cedeo de Fernández. Back then, she was the First Lady of the country.

From then on, my life began to have a radical change. For those who used to see me in my community as the least lonely and bored child, now they see me as an example to follow.

Those who today say that you will not be someone in life will be the first ones to tell you tomorrow that they knew you were going to succeed. Guess what? I graduated with high honors from high school. After that, things began to change. Once you start loving yourself, you will be able to love others. If you think you're worthless, you're not loved, or you do not love yourself, then it's impossible to give love. How can you give love if you're worthless? What value will your love have?

I have lost important people in my life, but I have come across great friends that I have always loved.

I have learned something from each of those friends, even from those who thought they had nothing to teach me.

I have been living not the life of others, with fame, a lot of money, and those who believe in consumerism, but my own life. That's why I have nothing to envy anyone, for I know that I am doing what I have to do.

Do not do what people expect of you, but only what makes you feel fine with yourself, what you really want. Believe me when I say that you can have wealth, a life free of bad habits, be intelligent, expressive, sophisticated, successful in studies and business... in short, you can be the most important person in the world, but if you do not live authentically, you are nothing.

NATIONAL SPELLING BEE COMPETITION

At age 20, I undertook a trip to Santiago for a new stage: the university. I enrolled in medical school at the State University of the Dominican Republic (UASD). At first, I had nowhere to stay, and this was the first bitter experience I encountered away from my mother's house. A cousin of a friend of my mom's had sheltered me, but this would cost me psychological trauma. Over time, that person began to feel uncomfortable with my presence in the house. Therefore, I had no other option than to leave the house in search of another place to stay. Hopefully, a good-hearted man named Aquilino, the executive head of the fire department of a Santiago city hall called La Canela, allowed me to stay at the fire station for as long as I wanted. I could not complain of such hospitality. I stayed there for a month and then moved into a boarding house. It was my own decision due to the unbearable noise of the truck siren, which was constantly playing music in my ears every time there was an emergency.

If you want to discover the power that is within you, you must first be ready to face the difficulties that you will encounter in life. For the first time in my life, I felt this independence in the boarding house.

During my short stay in that city hall, I met a family, the Pilarte family; they welcomed me as a son. I also met Mrs. Bertha, who still loves me as her own son. So far, I have maintained a close relationship as mother-son with both the Pilarte family and Mrs. Bertha. While I was living there, I was studying two careers: medicine at the state university previously mentioned (UASD) and English at the University of ISA (with a scholarship), in the Dominican Republic. After graduating from English with the highest honors, the MESCYT (Ministry of Education, Science and Technology) awarded a scholarship with full payment to go to the state university of Utah, United States, in order to master my English.

If you are still alive, it is because God has a plan for you. So, NEVER GIVE UP!

In fact, God will bless you in such a way that many will regret having once rejected you in their lives.

Find the purpose of your life.

When I came back from the United States, I was instantly appointed as an English teacher at ISA through the English Immersion program. Do not let the circumstances make you change your name. The difference between you and success lies in the sacrifice.

Due to the little time invested in my medical career, I had to resign from my job as a teacher so that I was able to stay focused on my medical studies. In a short time, I was recognized as a meritorious student in the UASD, and from there I was allowed to assist some professors in the subject of Applied Anatomy. Technically, I was teaching the other guys there!

Make every moment of your life count. Don't waste your time.

If there is something you should be good at, it is believing in yourself, period.

MERITORIOUS STUDENT AT THE AUTONOMOUS UNIVERSITY OF SANTO DOMINGO VENUE SANTIAGO (UASD-SANTIAGO)

Never forget who you are.

Once you know your position, you can always change your life condition.

Tell me who your friends are, and I will tell you who you are. I have met positive and negative people along the journey of my life, but I am the one who decided who to be with. Today we have a language institute called American Accent English School, of which I am the head master.

Everything has been possible thanks to the ideas of my doctor friends, Jean and Gerald; these ideas were converted into actions immediately.

If you want something, fight for it. Period. If you spend most of your time watching television or chatting, you will not discover the giant within you. Don't waste your time. As my mentor says, we are running out of time.

What are you going to do with the time you have left?

Currently, I am working on a project where we record audio and videos of self-improvement and personal growth so that valuable people can listen to and watch stories that motivate and change lives because we all have potential; it just takes a little bit of motivation.

I have seen people with less talent than others, but they use their time correctly.

Excuses are the tools of the weak. Never say you cannot, because that goes to the subconscious and is going to take root, and then there will be no room for positive thoughts. Today I say with joy that I am a doctor and I owe everything to God, to my decision to persevere and fight, and to my family.

It is time to change! If you ask me how, I will tell you that it is a combination of your attitude and decision towards change.

The lion is not the biggest animal in the jungle (the elephant is).

The lion is not the tallest (the giraffe is); it is not the most intelligent (the rabbit and the monkey are); and neither is it the heaviest (the hippopotamus). However, when it makes an appearance, all the other animals run for their lives.

The Lion is the leader of the jungle by a single word: Attitude.

My mother, colleagues, friends, and my professor, Juan Guerra Rodrguez,

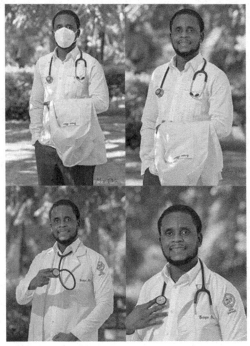

CHAPTER 2
BECOME THE PERSON
THAT NO ONE THOUGHT
YOU COULD BE!

Perhaps you are going through difficult times, but keep the faith and when they ask you how you are, keep firmly declaring that you are blessed and prosperous because you are under the grace of God. Every time you say it, you will see the glory of God upon you.

When you are in a very unfortunate situation, do not take the presence of that problem to indicate the absence of God. Sometimes, when you face an intangible storm, nobody but you will know. Hence, it requires emotional intelligence to deal with something internal. Has anyone gone through a secret storm? When you are the only one aware of what is happening to you, it is difficult to convince others that you are immersed in something that is burning you and harming you inside.

Do not let circumstances force you to change your name.

There is a price that we have to pay for each level that one reaches in life, so no one should feel jealousy or envy for the success of another person; they do not know what it has cost you to have that success. What will you do with the time you have left? I assure you that if you do not evaluate yourself, you could lose the best moment of your life, because it is time to change the way we think about things and the way we face problems.

Today is your best moment to discover the giant that lives inside of you. If you want to go through an evolutionary scale, you must have the courage to deal with pressure and social criticism. It is evident that the new challenges will bring new problems, but we have to be strong to withstand those problems.

When you're making progress, everyone wants to be like you, even though no one knows the efforts and sacrifices you had to make; the only thing most people focus on is your present, but you had to go through a difficult past first. The difference between your present and the past was then marked by that past. In other words, your perspective should be the fruit of your retrospective life and then improve your prospective condition. If you do not improve your past, you will be prone to repeating the same problems in the future. No one has said that it would be easy to deal with problems. Based on my personal life, I know that it is not easy to get up with empty pockets and, to make matters worse, with the worry of paying the bills of electricity, water, the rent of the house, the internet, the debts of the bank and other creditors, it's hard. But, how do we conceive of those moments and how do we handle them? Just stop and think a little, calmly, because you have all kinds of tools and the formula for these problems in your mind. It depends on you and your capacity for rationalization.

If you know who you are, then you also know who you are not. If you do not know who you are, someone can give you an identity and you will become what they want you to be, and that is what has happened to many of us. Some of us have wanted to imitate or have imitated other people, sometimes through the influence of these people, because we do not know who we are. We become what they want us to be, and then, when they leave us, we are confused because we do not have an understanding of their modus *vivendi* or of who we really are. Imagine you have a bank account where you deposit $86,400 every morning. The account does not transfer balance day by day; it allows you to keep the balance in cash, and every night you cancel any part of the amount that you have not used during the day. What would you do? Take out every dollar day by day? We all have a bank like that; its name is Time. Every morning, it credits you with 86,400 seconds. Each night you write down, as if lost, any time that you could not use wisely. It does not take balance from day to day, and it does not allow overdrafts, so you cannot borrow against yourself or use more time than you have.

Every day, the account starts fresh. Every night, you destroy an unused time slot. If you do not use the deposits of the day, it is your loss and you cannot appeal to recover it. There is never a loan period. You cannot take out a loan against your time or against another person's. The time you have is the time you have and that's it.

Time management is yours to decide how to spend your time. As with money, you decide how to spend it. What will you do with the time you have left?

Night and day, you talk about success, you dream of succeeding, you want to succeed, but what are you doing to be successful? The difference between you and success lies in sacrifice. Do not limit yourself, and do not listen to the naysayers (negative voices). If you believe in yourself, you will win. Dare to dream and make your dreams a reality!

No one can understand your success until they understand your struggles. Mark Fisher once said that some of us repeat that we will never succeed because we come from a family of losers or because we have had failures that, in our eyes, seem to be definitive. So, we go from failure to failure, not because we do not have the qualities required to succeed, but because that is how we unconsciously think we are.

Make the impossible a reality. Think big and dare to accomplish your projects because the size of a project depends on you. A story with a happy ending first requires a bitter half. This is what the road to success is like. I assure you that if there is something you should be good at, it is believing in yourself, because those who say that you will not be someone in life will be the first to tell you tomorrow that they knew you were going to succeed, that you were going to go far, and that you were going to make a difference.

If you want to be successful, remember never to give up and always believe in yourself despite the repeated setbacks, for God will bless you in such a way that many will regret having once rejected you in their lives, because impossible is nothing for God.

The road to success requires sacrifices. Each fight is worth it.

Listen carefully: NEVER allow anyone to tell you that you are too small to become big.

CHAPTER 3
AN INDELIBLE
EXPERIENCE

Many of us wander in the world without a clear direction or purpose. We live in a world of fantasies, a mere imagination, a utopia... It's good to dream, but it's much better to put every dream into action. A dream without an action plan will always be a dream. I remember that day as if it were today, the day I had to miss class because I did not have money for the fee transportation to go to the university. Everything was literally dark; my soul was not like before. It was a Wednesday, around 8:00 A.M. It was one of those days where the day-to-day struggle was the main occupation. Since I don't usually like begging for money, the previous day I meditated on the next day, about how to get at least the money to go to class. Unfortunately, no sign of hope was seen. When I woke up that morning, hopeless, the only thing I did was cry, and I had no choice but to call my brother with an anguished and worrying voice. After a few minutes, I realized that the message had been transmitted; this little problem was already taken care of immediately. It may sound a bit unusual, but despite having good relations with my mother and brothers, I had been idealized as an independent dude. When life hits you really hard and you want to give up, think twice. You will notice that you are a miracle of God.

Living your dream or giving up does not cost the same price. Giving up has a very high price. Living our dreams allows us to share the miracle of life, and renouncing them takes us away from everything that is exciting and essential.

When I finally got money for schooltransportation, the first thing I did was catch up with the missing class and the topic for the next class session. My biggest concern has always been not missing class, because it is not easy to make up for lost time.

Throughout my life, I tried to maintain a way of life full of humility; I was taught that offending others is not for civilized beings.

During the early phase of my career, I met people of all kinds, but I always handled myself with caution.

At first, everything was fine. The relationship between my colleagues and I was similar to a family relationship. We are actually prone to living like family when it comes to medical students, for we will always be sharing and seeing each other very often, right? Unfortunately, all of that was a momentary experience. Medical school at the UASD is divided into a basic cycle: pre-medical, medicine, pre-internship, and internship. Throughout this entire long path to the end, there is a lot to see and know about who your true friends are or are not. To make a long story short, though, there are things that cannot be said. With all this said, you might understand what I am talking about by reading between the lines. Have you ever had friends or classmates/colleagues who are only with you because they are looking for the same goal as you are, and when the goal has been reached, they leave you? Well, that is what has happened to me. Without any further ado, let me take you on a quick reading tour from the root of this issue in order for you, as readers, to understand what has really happened to me. Take heed, there are three types of friends: confidants, who are with you in your ups and downs, they fight with you the good fight and cry with you when you have to cry. They also laugh with you if necessary; the next type of friends are the constituents. They are only with you to exploit you. They help you spend but not to recover, and, once they have absorbed everything, they leave you; and the last kind of friends are the comrades. They are with you to fight for the same goal. Once the objective has been met, it is possible that they do not appear: the famous semester companions. The former is my kind of colleague. Getting back to the main point of this paragraph, that is one of the reasons why I have completely changed with the majority of my so-called old college friends. The need for approval from others is equivalent to saying: "what you think of me is more important than the opinion I have of myself."

CHAPTER 4
DO NOT SHOW RESISTANCE TO CHANGE

"Progress is impossible without change, and those who cannot change their minds, cannot change anything."
George Bernard Shaw

Elizabeth Obih-Frank once asked, "Do you think that people can change?" Why the change? We have to. Every human being has been or has to go through a transition in their lives sooner or later, because it is the natural progression of every living being to undergo a change. Like it or not, change, like death, is inevitable. When we are less open to change, everything becomes less favorable and we feel that nothing is going the way we want. Fear is what often gets in the way and hinders our efforts to embrace change. When we are more open to change, we only do it if we think that there will be more advantages than disadvantages, or simply when we have experienced all the options and are willing to try a new approach or path. In both cases, fear is a dominant characteristic factor. The irony is that we often say, "I am open to change." But, in reality, most of us are only open to change if we can control the terms and conditions.

CHAPTER 5
THE PATH TO SUCCESS

The success of a person depends, in whole part, on the way they handle adversity in life, and one of the phrases that echoes in my mind is that adversity is a fact of life.

When faced with an unexpected event, we can abandon and adopt a novice attitude, or else we can interpret that unforeseen circumstance as an opportunity to find other ways of doing things. We can be determined, persistent, and perseverant. It all comes down to your choice, and it's an attitude choice!

The difference between those who always fight to reach the goal and those who finally surrender simply relies on the desire to excel. It is a matter of being either optimistic or pessimistic, per se.

To give an example, there are people who have had to live a life with limited opportunities, bitterness, financial poverty, and social havoc, but they never give up. On the other hand, there are others who give up on the first attempt if they see that they have failed during that first try.

Life is not about who is going to arrive or not, but who is going to maintain it once it has arrived at the top. Nobody said that our existence was going to be easy. Therefore, you will have to start developing your capacity for resistance and your ability to overcome problems constantly. Always stay in the search for solutions.

Of course, if a problem has no solution, why worry? And if there is a solution, why worry? Worry creates stress, and then you will gradually wear out.

CHAPTER 6
LEARNING TO MAKE DECISIONS

"The most important obstacle that man must overcome in order to achieve the goals and the state he intends for his life is found on his inner side."

We may not always be able to choose the level of difficulty with which we must contend, but we can choose how to respond if this is the case. Every human being has the ability to face and solve a problem. Everything depends on the path he or she chooses. We are aware of our actions and, in chemistry, this would result in a reaction that could translate the product of the stimulus that gave rise to them. Everything that happens has to happen, in an avoidable or inevitable way.

This is a fact. The secret to any eventuality is to work to minimize the consequences that it brings and to maximize the abilities of emotional intelligence. When you are able to reduce your emotional reactions to a situation, you can directly or indirectly deal with the problem in a constructive way.

Every adversity, every failure, and every pain of the heart carries the seed of an equal or greater benefit. Napoleon Hill

Although life seems to be difficult sometimes, never give up because things will change. An arrow can be thrown only when pulled back. When life drags you back with difficulties, it means that it is going to throw you into something big.

Just stay focused and keep aiming. If you fail, you will fall next to the stars. Do not complain that your problems are too big. Better focus on taking advantage of the problems since adversity creates opportunity.

When I have problems, my philosophy is this: I do not tell people because 80% do not care and the remaining 20% are happy that I am in trouble. In spite of everything, EVERY PROBLEM HAS A SOLUTION. BE WISE AND FIND THE SOLUTION.

Fix your sight in five directions: up, to see where you are; down, to see who you're stepping on; on the sides, to see who is extending a hand; Backward to see where you're coming from and forward to see where you're going.

CHAPTER 7
PROFESSOR SUBSTITUTE
AT UASD-SANTIAGO

If you do not want to have most people as enemies, just be an ordinary person.

There are differences between people who like your way of being and those who love you as you are, or vice versa. At the beginning of this story, I mentioned that I was helping a professor in the field of applied anatomy. This experience, despite its great benefits in the acquisition of knowledge, has also been a bitter pill. To be an official monitor (someone in charge of a class session), it is mandatory to compete. However, a professor can have you as his assistant without the need to compete if you are really good at a subject. This, along with my first confrontation with respect to the change of a class schedule, has intensified the bad relationship between my colleagues and me. They had a nickname for me: "nié" (it grammatically means "neither... nor"). The fruits spoke for themselves. I understand that I was not an official monitor, but it was not because I could not, rather there was no contest assigned for campuses outside of the capital of the country back then. When our circumstances change, our minds also do. Some people may be unable to see how things were previously and may fail to appreciate them. I learned to be a lonely boy and live life as I was born: naked and alone.

CHAPTER 8
MY BELIEF IN GOD

"What I know for sure is that nothing is for sure."
TD Jakes, Bishop

It is possible that my devotion to God has not been perceived among so many lines and writings, but I must admit that I am madly in love with the Supreme Being, Jesus Christ. Since I was born until now, I have cultivated certain religious and human values that persist even today.

Science may deny His existence and claim that my faith in Jesus is based on ignorance, but you cannot undo what He has done for me. I remember those times when schools and Sunday services arrived and my mom, a selfless woman in God's service, was always actively awake to make sure we were motivated and ready to go to church.

There are certain moments in your life that are worth living twice. For example, having been inculcated with biblical principles has allowed me to meditate before acting. When I say meditate, I refer to a manifestation of patience, good sense, and justice before making a decision. Therefore, it was worthwhile to be born into a Christian family.

As a way to encourage people to read the Bible, a man devised a Bible reading contest. By then, when I was only 17 years old, I started reading so much of the Bible that I had already read it through twice. I used to get up with it in my hands and with my eyes wide open. When I returned from work, it was the first thing I thought of, but over time, everything had changed.

After the transition from adolescence to adulthood, the new responsibilities were limited, and there was a gradual lack of interest in reading the Holy Scriptures. As a result, I can still feel the side effects of not maintaining the same reading rhythm as it used to be before.

One of the psalms that I like to read and meditate upon is Psalm 91. I quote:

Psalm 91: New International Version (NIV)
Whoever dwells in the shelter of the Most High
They will rest in the shadow of the Almighty. [a]
2 I will say of the Lord, "He is my refuge and my
    fortress.
    My God, in whom I trust."

3. Surely he will save you.

> From the fowler's snare
> and from the deadly pestilence.

4: **He'll envelop you in his feathers.**

> And you will find refuge under his wings;
> His faithfulness will be your shield and rampart.

5: **You will not be terrified by the terrors of the night.**

> Not the arrow that flies by day,

6 or the pestilence that stalks in the darkness,

> Neither the plague that wreaks havoc at midday

7: **A thousand people may fall by your side,**

> ten thousand dollars in your right hand,
> but it will not come near you.

8 **You will only be able to observe with your eyes.**

> and see the punishment of the wicked.

9 If you say, "The Lord is my refuge,"

> And you will you make the Most High your dweling,
> **No** harm will overtake you.
> No disaster will come near your tent.

11 **For he will give orders to his angels concerning you.**

> to protect you in all your endeavors;

12), they will lift you up in their hands.

> so that you will not strike your foot against a stone.

13: **You will walk over the lion and the cobra.**

> You will trample the great lion and the serpent.

14. Because he [b] loves me," says the Lord, "I will rescue him;
I will protect him because he acknowledges my name.
15 He will summon me, and I will respond;
I will be with him in trouble.
I will deliver him and honor him.
16. With long life, I will satisfy him.
and show him my salvation."

Undoubtedly, there is nothing better than looking for the presence of God and walking with Him because nothing is safe in life and our existence is like a lightning bolt. So, I extend a special invitation to all readers who have this book in their hands so that they can learn more about God and know him fully. I repeat my phrase from TD Jakes, "What I know for sure is that nothing is safe."

CHAPTER 9
ENGLISH TEACHER

Always try to do your best in everything you do. If you have to travel an extra mile, do not think twice, just do it.

Monday, January 16, 2012, a memorable date as if it were today, was the moment when I officially started taking my English classes. The Ministry of Education, Science, and Technology *(MESCyT)* granted me a scholarship to study English at ISA through the English Immersion Program (a twelve-well designed English learning program offered by the Dominican government).

As indicated previously, I was taking both English and medicine classes simultaneously. At first, I was like a fish out of water, but it did not take me a month to get the hang of the English class. My prior Basic English level most likely helped me shine among the best, because three months later, I was at the top of my class. Despite the difficult times, rainy weather, and med school, I never missed any of my 6 to 10 pm English classes, although I commuted approximately 32 miles every day from Monday to Friday, back and forth from my house to the university and then from there to my English classes. I knew that the result of that daily routine of mine was somehow worth it. After having completed six months in the program, the *MESCyT* gave us the first written and oral evaluation, and, as expected, I was one of the ones with the highest score. As the Bible says in 1 John 5:14, I quote: "This is the confidence we have in approaching God: that if we ask according to his will, he hears us."

There are teachers that make a difference in one's life. There I met my teacher, Nicolas Rodriguez, an honest and kind man. His honesty was perceptible, and his kindness was incomparable. He used to give me a ride every night right after class was over. I also met the coordinator, Kelvin Vasquez, a humble and fair man. From a motivational point of view, he helped me a lot. He used to take me as an example to motivate other students. He told them that in addition to dedicating time to med school, I also did it with English class, and I did well in both studies.

Due to the fact that I had started med school with an ear scholarship from *MESCyT*, I was informed that this same higher education ministry also has a program offering mini-laptops to all the scholars. Since I did not have a laptop back then, I loved that idea, and I did not wait any longer to have my laptop requested. My request was successfully approved, and a unique date was assigned to pick up the laptop. I was in class, and the next day was the big day to receive my first laptop, but there was a problem: I did not have the money for transportation to go to Santo Domingo. It was 8:04 P.M. and we had a class breakfast. I was pacing up and down with a deep concern since the next day was important to me, but the problem of the bus roundtrip ticket was not yet solved. When we got back to the class after the break, I called my teacher, Nicolas, aside for a minute and explained my situation to him. He understood and recommended that I announce it to the group. At first, I felt a little bit uncomfortable and embarrassed, but I had no other choice.

Minutes after standing up and explaining the problem to my classmates, I was really shocked, yet I had gotten the round-tripbus ticket thanks to them. I felt a joy inside of me and a firm desire to energetically continue with my studies. After that unexpected experience, I noticed that everything we want can be achieved if we have faith. Surely, the next day, I went to Santo Domingo to pick up the computer. As of today, I still keep it with me, which means it is my external brain: I have all kinds of information stored in it.

It was already December, and it was time to graduate from the English school, upon completion of the whole learning process. As predicted, I was one of the chosen ones to go to Utah State University (USU) in order to master that language. I received the news with great devotion and distinction.

Evidently, we went to the United States. The experience was extraordinarily unique, and as a result, I not only learned about American culture, but that trip also changed my way of thinking and seeing things. I learned over there that acceptance is the basis of cultural and ethnic differences. Upon returning from there, I was instantly an English teacher in ISA.

Dear Reader, I have seen people with less talent than you, but doing more than you. Invest more time in yourself and never give up. When you believe in yourself, the impossible becomes possible because there is greatness within you and, if you do not believe me, ask Les Brown.

Utah State University is located in the United States of America.

English Instructor in the English Immersion Program at ISA

CHAPTER 10
INSTITUTE OF LANGUAGES AMERICAN ACCENT ENGLISH SCHOOL-AAES

One of the reasons why the poor are poor is because they are not educated enough to identify the opportunity to be an entrepreneur.

It is always good to think big and aspire to the impossible. The vicissitudes gave me many reasons to give up, but I always saw more reasons to continue fighting and never give up.

Nobody said that life was going to be easy. Impossible is nothing, though. Given that I was leading a double life, I had to quit my job as a way to focus more on med school. Honestly, it was a very difficult decision because of my limited financial resources. Focusing entirely on studying without a source of income has been a challenge that has taught me the value of my existence.

After that tough decision, what I did was get a temporary job every semester and quit before I reached three months in the positions assigned. By law, an employee has a 90-day probation period, so I never wanted to last that time. The only thing that I wanted was to get some money to keep up with the semesters.

Due to my work performance in several "call centers," I have gotten a wide range of experience in customer service and sales due to my work performance in several "call centers." I did everything for a good cause: to study medicine.

Over time, he had enough money to take a break from work and study more.

Now that I had more free time, I invested my time in libraries. Next to my house is a private university named UTESA. Its library was my second home for study purposes only. I was eventually able to meet all kinds of potential students. During one of my study sessions there, I met two good medical students: Jean-T. Joassaint and Gerald Lee. It did not take us too long to found an entity called FUJEP, whose acronym means *"Fuerza de Unidad de JóvenesEmpresarios para el Progreso"*. At first, it was idealized by Dr. Joassaint and me. But then Mr. Lee was invited and immediately became part of the association. Through several collective ideas and projects in the short and long term, we started with the foundation of the language institute called American Accent English School-AAES.

Like any other project, this was not easy, but God has helped us shape the way with the local place and publicity. Our language academy has had significant growth, and our students are grateful to us.

CHAPTER 11
SOCIAL SERVICES

"What kind of meaning does his/her life have if he/she does not live to serve?"

I constantly and firmly utter the following: "If you do not live to serve, what kind of meaning does your life have?" We are born for a purpose and, unless we discover the reason for our existence, we will not know why we live.

When I was little, I used to see missionaries from different countries go to my community, providing social assistance or doing charitable works. The residents of my community benefited a lot from medical operations, the provision of food and clothing, you name it. The missionaries were, for the most part, Americans. Therefore, that was one of the reasons why I learned English so fast. The communication between them and the people of my community was very poor and linguistically limited, for their interpreters were not enough for so many people either.

At first, I was very shy and did not want to go near them, but over time, I faced my fear and talked.

These people were just trying to help, so there was an instant friendship connection. A few times, I was already one of the interpreters. When I moved to Santiago for the reasons already explained, my goal was always to find a way to help my community. As a medical student, I always saw doctors and professors organizing medical operations.

I even volunteered so that, in this way, I was able to acquire knowledge and develop a sense of self-commitment in the area. That way, I would, of course, organize my own free clinical consultation there. He had accumulated sufficient knowledge on the subject over time, which led him to establish the organization "For a Child" (now known as M.E.D.I.C.O.S). It is a bit unusual, but although the specific objective is focused on children, we also have general objectives that encompass both pediatric and adult populations. Today, we have already gone to several places in the country to organize medical operations. In addition to this, we also provide food, clothing, and toys to the populations consulted. The idea is to reach the neediest homes and give a smile to each person with whom we have physical contact. When we learn that it is better to give than to receive, we will begin to live in and have a better world.

Toy distribution in Batey la GRUA

A MEDICAL OPERATION was performed in La Gracia, Ibbert.

PADRE GRANERO, PUERTO PLATA, CONDUCTS A MEDICAL CONSULTATION

CHAPTER 12
WHAT'S NEXT

As the journalist Manuel Toro Galea says, in life, there are certain moments in which it is difficult to move forward. We are sometimes in the middle of some tough situations where we need a pushup to be able to face the problems and not fall in the attempt. There are people who have gone through these circumstances and live to tell the world their experiences so that what they have been through can be a source of inspiration and help to others. They are mortal human beings like you and me, who have a normal life, but one day something happens to them. Their lives, from that point, have been radically different. Instead of feeling sorry, they go ahead and leave us with stories to reflect on personal improvement.

Nick: no arms, no legs, and no limits.

Due to an illness, Nick Vujicic was born in Melbourne (Australia) in 1982 and came into the world without limbs. Despite the limitations, Nick has managed to skydive, be cast in short films, write a best-seller (no legs, no arms, and no worries), play football and golf, become a great speaker, get married and have children.

Nick is content: he does not dwell on what he lacks, but is grateful for what he does have, for who he is, and he sets aside his fears. What Nick transmits is that it is necessary to accept life as it comes, knowing that we can achieve what we want with effort and perseverance.

With this, he tries to make us understand that everything is possible and that we should never give up in life. If he can, anyone else can do it.

Malala, the survivor

She won the Nobel Peace Prize in 2014. At the age of 17, she was the victim of a terrorist attack and managed to survive after several operations in which her life was in danger. To this day, she is fighting for human rights; she is dedicated to promoting equality and trying to solve the problems of her country of origin, Pakistan.

She appears often on various television programs and has a blog that is known throughout the world. The bullets that wounded her changed her life radically, but did not diminish her determination to fight so that girls in Pakistan have access to education.

Oliver, the photographer with Down Syndrome,

Oliver Hellowell is a boy who, at 18, dreams of becoming a professional photographer. His nature photographs are known all over the world and have thousands of followers on Facebook. At birth, he was diagnosed with Down's syndrome and had problems learning the language, but he has become an athlete who has found in photography a unique form of expression. He has learned to reflect in his photographs his sensitivity and his love for nature. Oliver is the perfect example that everything is possible.

Idrisand's perseverance to give their daughters a better future

The story of Idris was told by the Bangladeshi photographer GMB Akash on his Facebook page. Idris worked tirelessly cleaning sewers so his daughters could go to college. He did not tell his daughters what he was doing and was accumulating money to pay for his studies. On the day he had to pay the tuition, he did not have enough money because he had not been able to work that day, so his coworkers gave him all the money for that day and paid the tuition. Idris is an example of love and a firm will to give his daughters a better future despite the circumstances.

Stephen Hawking: The Genius with ALS

We all know him, his theories and his story. This physicist and cosmologist was diagnosed with ALS at the age of 20, but that has not stopped him from developing his theories about spatio-temporal singularities, black holes, or what is known as Hawking radiation. ALS has been aggravating his health over the years until he has completely remained paralyzed and in a wheelchair. But that has not stopped him from continuing to study and work. His best-known informative work is A Brief History of Time. If you want to know his history, you can see the movie "The Theory of Everything," which is about his life and his illness.

Narayanan Krishnan, the chef who feeds the poor

Nobody doubted his skills as a chef when he worked in a 5-star hotel in Switzerland. One day, he traveled to his hometown in India, Madurai, and saw something that changed him completely: an old man who had no food, ingesting his own excrement. From that moment, Narayanan knew that he must do something. He fed the old man and left his job to found the NGO Akshaya Trust, which serves millions of meals to elderly people who are disabled and abandoned on the street. Today, he feeds about 400 people a day.

Thomas Edison, the apprentice of failure.

I have not failed. I've only come across 10,000 ways that do not work. "This is the famous phrase of Thomas Edison, the inventor who has most contributed to changing our lives. He patented more than 1,000 inventions and never gave up. He learned from his failures and always knew that he would find the right solution. His motivation was inexhaustible, and he taught us to keep going.

Charles Chaplin: humor and love

Charlot was the creator of one of the most memorable, loved and tender characters in the world of cinema: Charlot. He used humor to make a critique of capitalism and the dehumanization that lived and still lives in the world today. At the beginning, he was rejected by the film executives because they thought he would not like it, and that his work was strange. The character of Charlot debuted in 1914 with the film *"Ganándose el pan"* (earning bread), and only during that year 35 short films were shot. His best-known films are The Chimera of Gold, City Lights,

Modern Times, and The Great Dictator. Chaplin became one of the most famous actors in Hollywood.

Soichiro Honda, the defiant entrepreneur

Soichiro Honda went to Toyota to conduct a job interview to cover a free vacancy. Apparently, his profile was not very funny to the company, and they decided that Soichiro was not the right person for the position. What is it that he did? He created a company that competed with Toyota, to which he gave his surname.

Kelvin Doe, the engineer from Sierra Leone,

This young man from Sierra Leone had to live in a place with a shortage of opportunities. His future could have been to become one of the famous child soldiers who have so much to talk about. His story begins with the dream of building his own radio. For this, the young man would start studying engineering on his own in 2010. In 2012, Kelvin had already managed to appear on major television networks such as CNN and BBC, as well as become the youngest guest to enter the visitor program of the Massachusetts Institute of Technology.

All the reflecting stories teach us something: they keep a secret that tells us that we cannot give up, that there is always a reward at the end of the road. Overcoming adversities, achieving what we want, knowing ourselves and overcoming our barriers and fears is what moves us, what makes us improve ourselves every day as people and as professionals. We just have to dare to leave our comfort zone to start flying.

CHAPTER 13
IN STORIES THAT I HAVE
BEEN AFFECTED BY
IN A POSITIVE WAY

When I arrive home from the hospital or finish teaching a language class session, I sit in my room and start reading stories. The ones that most appeal to me are the following:

I

He was driving at full speed in his new sports car without any precautions. He suddenly heard a thunderous knock on the door, stopped, and, when he got off, saw that a brick had ruined his luxurious car. He saw a little boy and grabbed him by the arms and pushed him towards his car. He shouted, "It's a new car and that brick that you threw is going to cost you dearly!" Why did you do that? I'm so sorry, sir. "I threw the brick because nobody stopped." "He's my brother. He derailed his wheelchair. He fell on the ground and I cannot lift him." Can you, please, help me sit him in his chair? He is beaten and he weighs a lot for me alone. The executive swallowed a thick knot that had formed in his throat. Excited by what had just happened, he lifted the young man from the floor, seated him again in his chair, and took out his silk handkerchief to clean a little the cuts of that special boy's brother. After verifying that he was well, he looked at the boy, and he thanked him with a great, indescribable smile. "God bless you, sir, and thank you very much," he said.

The man watched as the boy walked away, pushing his brother's heavy wheelchair hard.

The executive did not repair the door of the car, maintaining the crack made by the bricks to remind him that he should not go through life so distracted and so fast that someone has to throw a brick to get his attention.

II

During a lecture on the great differences between generations, a presumptuous student took the issue to explain to an elderly man sitting close to him why it is impossible for the older generation to understand his generation:

"You grew up in a different world, almost primitive," he said, loud enough to be heard around him.

Today's young people grew up with television, the internet, mobile phones, jet planes, and trips to space.

Our space probes have visited Mars.

We have ships with nuclear energy and electric and hydrogen cars. computers with light-speed processes... and more".

After a brief silence, the elder replied:

You're right, my son, we did not have those things when we were young.

So we invented them!

Now tell me, arrogant, what are you doing for the next generation?"

The applause was deafening!

III

They say that there was once a blind man sitting in a park with a cap on his feet and a sign that, written with white chalk, read: "PLEASE HELP ME, I AM BLIND."

An advertising creative that passed in front of him stopped and looked at a few coins in his cap. Without asking permission, he took the sign, turned it over, took chalk and wrote another ad. He put the piece of wood back on the blind man's feet and left.

In the afternoon, the creative came back to face the blind man who asked for alms. Now his hat was full of bills and coins. The blind man, recognizing his steps, asked him if he had re-written his poster and, above all, what he had written there. The publicist replied, "Nothing that is not as true as your ad," but in other words.

He smiled and went on his way. The blind man never knew, but his new sign read: WE ARE IN SPRING, AND... I CANNOT SEE IT.

IV

A university student went out one day to take a walk with a teacher, whom the students considered his friend because of his kindness to those who followed his instructions. As they walked, they saw on the way a pair of old shoes and assumed that they belonged to an old man who worked in the field next door and who was about to finish his daily duties. The student told the teacher: "Let's make a joke, hide the shoes and hide behind those bushes to see his face when he does not find them." My dear friend, the professor told him, we never have to have fun at the expense of the poor. You are rich, and you can give this man joy. Place a coin in each shoe and then we will hide to see how he reacts when he finds them. He did that, and they hid in the nearby bushes. The poor man finished his duties and crossed the land in search of his shoes and coat. As he put on his coat, he slid his foot into his shoe, but when he felt something inside, he bent down to see what it was and found the coin. Stunned, he wondered what could have happened. He looked at the coin, turned it over, and looked at it again. Then he looked around, everywhere, but nobody was visible. He put it in his pocket and put on the other shoe. His surprise was doubled when he found the other coin. His emotions overtook him, and he fell to his knees and looked up at the sky, expressing his heartfelt gratitude in a loud voice, speaking of his sick and helpless wife and children, who had no bread, and how, thanks to an unknown hand, they would not starve to death.

The student was deeply affected, and his eyes filled with tears.

Now, said the professor, are you not more pleased than if you had made a joke?

The young man replied, "You have taught me a lesson I will never forget. Now I understand something that I did not understand before: it is better to give than to receive."

V

A family had bought a new car with 0 miles. It was very fancy, with a beautiful look inside or out, the upholstery, the color, everything. The father loved that car. Their effort was there. The husband, his wife and their little boy, only 3 years old, went on a trip; arriving at a service station, the parents got off and left the child in the car, closing the doors... The child found a marker and began to write in all that upholstery, with great enthusiasm and love, as children are accustomed to doing their things in this condition. After a while, the parents arrived and seeing the painting, the father started to burst out in fury. Seeing his "beautiful upholstery" all grated, he began to hit the child in his hands and hit him violently... until they had to get the child out of his hands. The child was in such bad condition that they had to take him to the hospital.

The telephone rings at the family's home and the father answers... they were calling from the hospital. Things had gotten more complicated... The father introduced himself. He was notified that the child's hands had to be amputated and that there was no other possible option.

Entering the father into the room, wrapped in tears... the boy says, smiling... Hello, Dad... I learned the lesson... I will not do it again, Daddy... but please give me back my little hands! The father left that room and committed suicide...

Why do we give such importance to material things to the extent of hurting our loved ones?

One day I was born. One day I will die, and I will take nothing with me, but am I really living?

A house is made of rock and wood, and a home of love.

VI

On an airplane, while the flight was taking off, "a woman" insistently pressed the bell to call the stewardess: What is the problem, Ma'am? -Ask the hostess: "Don't you see?" I replied to the woman, "I was placed next to a dirty Indian." I cannot stand these people next to me. Don't you have another seat? Please calm down, says the stewardess. Almost all the seats are taken. But I will see if there is a place available. The stewardess walks away and comes back a few minutes later: Madam, as I thought, there is nowhere left free in the economy class. I spoke with the commander and he confirmed that there were no more available places in the economy class. However, we still have a place in first class. Before the woman could make the slightest comment, the stewardess continued: "It is quite unusual to allow a person from the economy class to sit in first class." But, given the circumstances, the commander finds that it would be scandalous to force someone to sit next to such a disgusting person. The passengers around us were watching the scene with outrage. Then, the stewardess, addressing the Indian, says: If the lord wishes, take your hand luggage, since a seat in first class awaits you. And the passengers, who witnessed the scene, were surprised: they raised their arms and applauded!

CHAPTER 14
YOUR LIFE IS MORE THAN
WHAT YOU CAN IMAGINE

"The best way to discover our potential is to be in trouble. I have discovered the giant that lives inside of me thanks to the hard life that I have lived."

It is not easy to get up at 5:00 a.m. to get to the hospital before 7:00 a.m. on a daily basisvoluntarily for a whole year, which is commonly known as the internship. After that, I have to come back to teach English from 4:00 p.m. to 10:00 p.m. and, finally, take a rest at 11:00 p.m., get to cook and then go to sleep at 1:00 a.m. Can you imagine it? It is not easy to deal with everything by oneself, but these moments had to happen to know what we are made of. The circumstance decides everything.

That same boiled water that softens a sweet potato is the same one that hardens an egg. So, we simply have to wait for our moment to start producing and reap fruit. Sometimes I have felt discouraged, without strength, hope and wanting to give up everything because, in my opinion, I thought that life was unfair only with me. However, I have noticed that there are people in worse conditions and way of life than me. That encourages me a little and inspires me to continue with my goals and dreams without giving up on them.

Maybe you are going through a bad time and you believe that life is no longer worth living, but if you are reading this book and, if it helps you, the character that is telling this story is real and he has gone through situations that few mortal beings have experienced. However, he has never given up and is excited telling his story.

There have been several times that I have suffered secretly, I have been verbally belittled, repeatedly rejected, socially excluded, and unfairly mistreated. But I have good news! In spite of everything, I have never given up. When others take the time to criticize you it is because they see something in you that they lack of, so be proud of your life because someone else, indirectly, is valued by your existence.

It is unfortunate to see how some young people waste their time and when they reach their old age (old), they will realize that, after so much time wasted; their result will be zero (0). Every human mind is brilliant and we must be good at something. Dedicate your time to what you are good at and you will have different results from zero (0).

Who told you that you will not be who you want to be? Challenge your inner negative self and plan your goals. Even if they tell you that you are crazy, become deaf today so that tomorrow you will be the successful dreamer. As José Ortega andCasset said, life makes sense when it is made an aspiration to not give up to anything. We have to know that the world can only be grasped through action and not contemplation.

The most powerful impulse, in the ascent of man, is the pleasure that his own ability produces. Let's enjoy doing what we do well, and having done it well, let's enjoy ourselves doing it better and, what we do not know, let's learn it and then enjoy learning from it. We will thus be better because we will have learned with joy.

Today's circumstance should not determine your future. You have the option to decide and turn the damage and injustice into the drivers of your triumph.

CHAPTER 15
FRAUD

Live every moment of your life as if it were your last breath because you may die bitter and regret the fact that you have not enjoyed it to the fullest. During the internship, I have learned to take things slowly. I did not use to go out often, drink some glasses of wine, watch movies, or go to the movies with friends, etc. ... but now I do all that with all the freedom and openness.

There was a very close friend of mine who had been scammed. He had invested all his savings in a business, but then it turns out he was penniless, just because the business where his money was, wentinto bankruptcy. Since then I learned to live today without the worry of mourning tomorrow, because tomorrow would be a new day and we will not know what it will bring. The poor friend could not enjoy his money, the result of his sweat and, unfortunately, that bitter experience left him traumatized.

Why do I take everything calmly? I have been a victim of fraud twice. Before being surprised, I will explain how and why I have innocently fallen in those tempting offers.

In 2015, justcame back from the United States, I started working as an English teacher in the English immersion program. There is nothing better than a well-paid job! Things were going so well for me financially that my savings and bank account were increasing in numbers. I did not have to worry about my university tuition fees, since this was already solvedwith the student scholarship that I had from the Superior Ministry of Science and Technology *(MESCyT)*. Having seen that my savings gradually increased in the bank, I had thought of starting a business, but there was a restaurant in the city of Santiago that sold Creole food whose owner had a cooperative-type business; although he denied that it was not a cooperative. When I heard about his business, it took me 6 months to analyze it and then I decided to invest my money there. The business consisted of investing an amount, minimum 10,000 Dominican pesos and the partners (investors) received 10% of the interest on their capital for a period of one year. I must emphasize that there were two types of partners: a passive partner (I was one of them), one who invested less than one million pesos; and an active partner, who invested an amount equal to or greater than the amount previously mentioned.

At first everything was fine. I received my interest per month without any complaint. His business was in full bloom in the city and, in such a short time, he already had a large number of partners, both passive and active. By the end of the contract year, the partners had the option to either withdraw their capital or leave it there and continue to receive interest. Well, without having learned of the internal failures of the business as far as the administrative part is concerned, the year had passed and I did not even have the interest to withdraw my capital. Unfortunately, the business went bankrupt and we all lost our money. That unexpected situation completely dominated me because months before, I had resigned my job, then for the last time I was without money ever since I became a teacher. I was affected emotionally, academically and personally. But over time I was recovering my strength, looking for another job that did not splice with my university schedule until I collected some money to survive. Thank God, that's how it was. I was back on my feet.

Another experience that has completely destroyed me was one that someone with whom I grew up, and I even went to his stepfather's church in the city hall of Imbert. I will reserve his name due to the respect I have for his parents. In the early 2018, already in the internship, someone writes to me by WhatsApp asking me to teach him English. I tell him that I live in Santiago and that if he is willing to travel from his town to Santiago, there would be no problem.

As he came to me and, instead of talking about the English class as the main topic, he came with me with a business plan called MKT coins from the Bitcoin family. It was an online business that gave weekly interests to the members according to the amount invested and, in addition, the members receive a referral fee, that's to say, the members received a bonus for each person who decide to start the business. It was a multi-level business, although he said it was a unilevel. It took me a while to digest the information because I had already learned my lesson in the a priori scam and I did not want to be so receptive.

He kept insisting and insisting and as he saw that I had many friends in social media, he told me that he would enroll me in the business with the minimum amount and it would be out of his pocket, so that I refer my friends. I accepted the deal and I was signed in with the minimum package. I started promoting the business with friends and after a short time I had already referred ten people.

In the business, the person entering receives weekly interest for a period of 12 weeks or 3 months, the capital is included. That is, in the payment that the member receives, part of this capital was also included in small portions until all the moneyis fully paidduring for a period of 12 weeks. I was making profit of this idea with ease, so I applied for a bank loan to make an investment in my languages institute "AMERICAN ACCENT ENGLISH SCHOOL. AAES." I asked him to be my guarantor, upon his arrival at the bank, he did not qualify due to an outstanding unresolved debt that he had. Well, I looked for another guarantor and my loan was finally approved. When he found out, he told me to invest everything in this online business he was in, then I could invest in the institute with what I was going to earn while I was in his business. An inner voice told me yes while another told me no. Finally, I decided to invest half and left the other half in my savings account. I had no doubt that I was going to be, once again, a victim of a scam. As I had imagined, he cheated me. He paid me the first three weeks without any problem, but in the fourth week he told me that the platform had technical problems. After having resolved the technical failures, he made another deposit, which would be the last one I shall ever see from him. The guy was gone from my sight. When

I noticed the degree of the situation, I went to talk to his parents, they called him, and then he tells me that he does not owe me anymore. Even worse, I was even threatened by him. I did not think that a person who calls himself a Christian would do such a thing. The scammer is still out because we had not signed any physical contract nor had I received any receipt; everything was verbal.

CHAPTER 16
YOUR SOCIAL ENVIRONMENT DEFINES YOUR PERSONALITY

You can choose who to talk to and share your secrets with, because your social environment says a lot about you and your personality. I, personally, spend more time with myself than with others and that does not mean that I am a narcissist or arrogant, I am simply avoiding problems. It should be noted that our personality makes us unique as a person, according to the great psychologists, psychiatrists and other specialists in human behavior. How many times have we met people who prefer to be alone than in bad company? But there comes the dilemma that if the one who spends a lot of time is only narcissistic or a normal being, that's why most people confuse my personality with my character. They think that way because they have already analyzed my attitude and assume that a "mass effect" can occur every time we talk. So, sometimes staying alone could be the best option. However, we must emphasize that we must not fall into pride, because the context in which we want to reach is based on a choice, not humiliation. Many have a tendency to belittle others due to their deficient cognitive level and, if that is what we are going for, we all have a limit in terms of the level of knowledge acquired and there may be another level higher than ones far as interpersonal relationship is concerned. Hence, there would be a big problem because if the person at a higher level chooses not to speak with one who has a lower level, we would talk very little; unless like-minded people appear.

In order for the environment to define its personality, it is necessary to be clear about the personality type of each individual and the environment in which he or she is. For all of this, the most important thing is to know oneself. So, we'll summarize the personality types below.

Every medical student has given subjects that speak of personality, such as Mental Health and Human Behavior, Psychology and Psychiatry and, we know very well that such personality defines an individual. Sigmund Freud, considered the father of psychoanalysis, speaks of personality by dividing it into a conscious part, a preconscious and finally an unconscious part.

From the structural point of view, we could mention that Mr. Freud also referred to an "It" (unconscious impulses and desires), which represents the pleasure principle; an "I" (controls activities of thought and reasoning), which would be the principle of reality, and the "Super I" (guardian of morality), which would be the ideal I or the way in which the person would like to be. But it turns out that Mr. Jung later appeared speaking of the types of people according to their attitudes. He mentions the type of extroverted, introverted, rational and irrational person. In the first type, it refers to the person who focuses on social life and the external world; in the second type, it is that person who concentrates on his own thoughts and feelings; the next type is that which regulates his actions by the functions of thought and feeling, and finally, it is this person who bases his actions on perceptions (sensations or intuition) successively. However, when the individual begins to have a permanent pattern of their internal experience and behavior that could harm their environment, this translates into something more complicated that is known as "personality disorder," divided into three major groups: Types A, B, C. In type A we could mention the paranoid disorder of the personality that has been a pattern of distrust of others; the schizoid personality disorder where the individual distances himself from social relationships; we have for type B the antisocial personality disorder that is characterized by contempt and violation of the rights of others; Borderline personality disorder is that person who is unstable in interpersonal relationships; the histrionic disorder of the personality is when someone seeks more attention than normal of the others; the narcissistic personality disorder is well known because most people show traits and even suffer without realizing it because it is a pattern of grandiosity and the need of the individual to seek admiration from others; we have from group C to the personality disorder by avoidance, there the individual avoid all kinds of activity that has to do with interpersonal relationships for fear of criticisms rejections, and finally we have the personality disorder by dependence is when the individual He believes he needs others to do everything. In short, of all those types of personality that we have just mentioned, with which one or which ones do you identify more and why? The answer depends only on you.

CHAPTER 17
EVERYTHING IN LIFE
MAKES SENSE

"Every day brings you new opportunities; be wise and take advantage of each of them."

While I was wandering in the main avenue in Santiago called *"Circunvalación Sur"*, I could see from afar a beautiful phrase reflected in the glass of the back of a bus that caught my attention. I quote, "We live in a society where 60% of people are saddened by your success, 30% question it, 9% are indifferent and maybe 1% are jubilant."

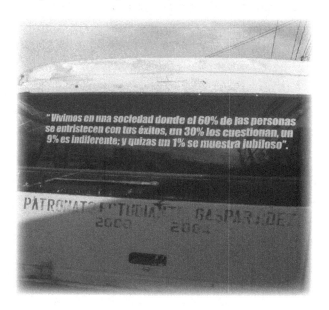

It is important to know to whom we tell our goals and dreams. Not everyone reacts in the same way to the success of others. When God sees your sufferings and decides to bless you, even the devil trembles and worries. To support this previous argument, Job is a very clear biblical example, so let's share a bit of his story below.

Job 1 New International Version (NIV)

1 In the land of Uz there lived a man whose name was Job. This man was blameless and upright; he feared God and shunned evil. 2 He had seven sons and three daughters, 3 and he owned seven thousand sheep, three thousand camels, five hundred yoke of oxen and five hundred donkeys, and had a large number of servants. He was the greatest man among all the people of the East.

4 His sons used to hold feasts in their homes on their birthdays, and they would invite their three sisters to eat and drink with them. 5 When a period of feasting had run its course, Job would make arrangements for them to be purified. Early in the morning he would sacrifice a burnt offering for each of them, thinking, "Perhaps my children have sinned and cursed God in their hearts." This was Job's regular custom.

6 One day the angels[a] came to present themselves before the Lord, and Satan[b] also came with them. 7 The Lord said to Satan, "Where have you come from?"

Satan answered the Lord, *"From roaming throughout the earth, going back and forth on it."*

⁸ Then the Lord said to Satan, "Have you considered my servant Job? There is no one on earth like him; he is blameless and upright, a man who fears God and shuns evil."

⁹ "Does Job fear God for nothing?" Satan replied. ¹⁰ "Have you not put a hedge around him and his household and everything he has? You have blessed the work of his hands, so that his flocks and herds are spread throughout the land. ¹¹ But now stretch out your hand and strike everything he has, and he will surely curse you to your face."

¹² The Lord said to Satan, "Very well, then, everything he has is in your power, but on the man, himself do not lay a finger."

Then Satan went out from the presence of the Lord.

¹³ One day when Job's sons and daughters were feasting and drinking wine at the oldest brother's house, ¹⁴ a messenger came to Job and said, "The oxen were plowing and the donkeys were grazing nearby, ¹⁵ and the Sabeans attacked and made off with them. They put the servants to the sword, and I am the only one who has escaped to tell you!"

¹⁶ While he was still speaking, another messenger came and said, "The fire of God fell from the heavens and burned up the sheep and the servants, and I am the only one who has escaped to tell you!"

17 While he was still speaking, another messenger came and said, "The Chaldeans formed three raiding parties and swept down on your camels and made off with them. They put the servants to the sword, and I am the only one who has escaped to tell you!"

18 While he was still speaking, yet another messenger came and said, "Your sons and daughters were feasting and drinking wine at the oldest brother's house, 19 when suddenly a mighty wind swept in from the desert and struck the four corners of the house. It collapsed on them and they are dead, and I am the only one who has escaped to tell you!"

20 At this, Job got up and tore his robe and shaved his head. Then he fell to the ground in worship 21 and said:

"Naked I came from my mother's womb,
    and naked I will depart.[c]
The Lord gave and the Lord has taken away;
    may the name of the Lord be praised."

22 In all this, Job did not sin by charging God with wrongdoing.

Although Job was in the midst of some tough trials, he never lost faith in God. And if we make an exegesis of this chapter of the book of Job, it could be inferred that the success of that righteous man in the eyes of God caused him trouble. Similarly, there are many people who do not want to see their neighbors progressing. But when these moments come, the first thing we should think about is God. God is the one who gives and also who takes away; everything that happens is because it had to be that way. In the same way, His name will be exalted.

CHAPTER 18
STIGMATIZATION

"Acceptance is the basis of differences"

I owe a lot to the Dominican Republic, the country that gave birth to me. There are no qualifying adjectives to express my love and gratitude to my people, a country with cheerful and friendly people. But I also have to express the bitter part that I have to live in some parts of the country simply because one is black. If I had to start writing my frustration as an individual who has to face pejorative expressions of other people towards me from day to day in the streets, I would already have several written volumes.

Some children (not all), from very young, already have their own concept and a learned perception of what, for them, means "blackness." Some call or consider the person of "black" skin as a strange individual, while others have special pejorative names that I do not want to quote; Everyone who was born and raised in this country knows what I mean. It is thought that everything that is black is bad, starting from black objects to human beings of that color. Nobody should accept that fact because the world was created for all and we all deserve to live in peace. Grow up with frustrations and live with the worry that if one day you will get up without being offended creates bad thoughts. I am a witness of how the blacks of some sectors of here, mainly the most marginalized neighborhoods, suffer verbal and even physical mistreatment and, all that is simply because of their skin color.

I know it every time I get into *"conchos"* (a public means of transportation), every time I listen to the news and every time I hear health personnel discriminating against pregnant women of Haitian descent. We cannot hide this reality; we cannot hide that reality on howlife is here. Again, not everyone thinks or acts with animosity. Once they get to know you, things dramatically change for good.

During my time as a student at the basic level, the most interesting topic was the part that spoke of the slavery of blacks and the expulsion of Haitians from this part of the island. Without lying, I felt frustrated and humiliated when they looked at me whenever they talked about some topic that belittlesthe people of color. One of my most recently experiences was thesentence 168-13 of the Constitutional Court that was an international explosion, because its objective revolves around the denationalization of every individual of Haitian descent born in The Dominican Republic.

In order for you to understand the previous point mentioned, let's talk a little deeper about the etiology of this decision made by the Dominican authorities. The Sentence 168-13 of the Constitutional Court established in 2013 that only persons born in Dominican territory of Dominican parents or legal residents are considered Dominican. The major concern of this decision was due to its retrospective and prospective consequences byapplying this law retroactively, dating from 1929 to 2010. This means that everyone who had a parent born here with an irregular status was considered in transit and, as a result, their children born will face deportation, since they do not have the birth right orwill enjoy the rights that the Dominican government had offered them for many years.

Obviously, this human right issue caught the attention of every one to the point that it went to the international level. As expected, that decision was massively and internationally rejected. A lot of convincing arguments have been uttered by the Dominican authoritiesin order to support that retroactive decision of theSupreme Court, however many intellectuals have interpreted it as a structural discrimination based on racial and ethnic criteria to the detriment of the people of Haitian descent migrants. Noting the marginalized situation that some children live in impoverished communities, with the mere fact of seeing the truncated dreams of those children, legally limited, and socially excluded; tears would come out of any rational human being's eyes.

It is understood that life is not easy, but living in a specific geographical place with few opportunities for personal growth and development, worsens the human way of life and, that could later lead an increase of the crime rate. Undoubtedly, you cannot fight crime if we do not attack the problem from its root and that lies in education. But despite that socio-economic gap of these children, you can see a constant and irradiated smile on their faces. If you want to have a closer look find out the way of life of these children, I invite you to take a walk in the *"bateyes"* and you will have a better understandingof this topic. Most of these people don't even have a formal job, because they are not endowed with legal documents. This is a human problem and I think there is a solution. Fortunately, the rate of these undocumented aliens has significantly decreased with the arrival of the Alien Regularization Plan, now many can somehow get by.

Many government leaders want to fight organized crime, corruption and socio-economic discrimination and the great cultural gap. Can this goal be achieved without education the people in the first place? I am referring to an education fostered in values and ethical principles as the most powerful weapon existing to eradicate the world's ills. When person is opposed tolearnhow to tolerate others, no matter how educated that person is, their education will not bring any good to humankind. In other words, there are fundamental human right violations. We can certainly bring out a change by taking the first step and starting to think about the well-being of today's children, regardless of their ethnic background or social class, so that they can be good leaders tomorrow. That change is now because if we educate children today, they will be examples to follow tomorrow.

CHAPTER 19
THE SCHOOL OF LIFE

"At school we learn the lesson and then we put that knowledge in the test, but in life we first go through the test and then we learn the lesson."

The internationally well-known Spaniard singer Julio Iglesias has a song that highlight the importance of flying high in life as eagles do because if you want to reach your goal, I don't think you'd like to go back to the miserable life you had. That's why I am going to repeat the same point from chapter 12, you have all kinds of tools within you to achieve what you want in life and, as a role model, it is always good to observe other people who were once in the basement like you, but now enjoying their success.

When you have observed enough all the characteristics that they are depicted by as successful people, you may not want to be like them, but at least you will be as successful as they are, because that is where the magic formula of life lies. They have paid a price. That price could have been high, average or low.

Now it's your turn to pay a price to get there and stay on top because everything that goes up can go down some day if one is neglected. But what happens when we have a bad experience or have lost everything we have achieved? In principle, we get frustrated and give a lot of mind to it, although that does not have to stay that way because, as a professor of mine of Psychiatry said, we ought to have resilience in order to have a new beginning, the courage to take and face the risks in life, patience before the situation and the restart, discipline to do what you like until you reach the goal and, more importantly, never stop being nice to others.

The idea is to never give up

No one said that life was going to be easy. Nelson Mandela lasted 27 years imprisoned before becoming the president of South Africa. It took Thomas Edison more than 10,000 attempts before inventing the electric bulb. Oprah Winfrey had a very impoverished childhood, however today she is not the same person. She is one of the most famous people in the world. J.W Rowling, the author of the Harry Potter book, had to wait long before her book was one of the best sellers. Bill Gates, being one of the richest in the world, did it without having obtained any university degree.

Of all these stories, the one that has moved me most is that of Chris Gardner and I will tell you as follows.

The story of Chris Gardner inspired the acclaimed film in *Search of Happiness*. He was an aspirant to be a stockbroker; he maintained a minimum salary and went through many difficulties. Gardner didn't even have enough money to pay for the down payment of his apartment. He even sometimeshad to sleep with his son Chris Jr, in the bathroom of a train station, in the parks, or under the desks in the office he was working at. Finally, Chris obtained the job of stockbroker in the firm called DeanWitter, and he founded his own investment company years later: Gardner Rich.

These are stories I am inspired by and even make me think twice before giving up. Failure is part of our lives. As much as we want to avoid failure, there is no way. We can fail in love, finances, in studies, etc... But the most important thing is to never give up. How many times have we had to suffer in secret? Many times we have had to start from scratch. Being left behind halfway is not an option.

Get up and move on despite all the difficulties! Stumbling and getting up is the best option, because at the end of the day one will be benefited from it.

Printed in the United States
by Baker & Taylor Publisher Services